IMAGES OF LONDON

EAST END
NEIGHBOURHOODS

IMAGES OF LONDON

EAST END
NEIGHBOURHOODS

BRIAN GIRLING

Frontispiece: Wellclose Square, Stepney, 1911. This picturesque neighbourhood of the old maritime East End once housed well-to-do ship's captains, but in later years commercialism and decay overwhelmed the square and demolition followed. Weatherboarded houses like these eighteenth-century examples once abounded in the inner East End but the twentieth century saw their demise. (Courtesy of LMA)

First published in 2005 by Tempus Publishing

Reprinted in 2009 by
The History Press
The Mill, Brimscombe Port,
Stroud, Gloucestershire, GL5 2QG
www.thehistorypress.co.uk

Reprinted 2010, 2011, 2012

British Library Cataloguing in Publication Data.
A catalogue record for this book is available from the British Library.

ISBN 978 0 7524 3519 0

Typesetting and origination by
Tempus Publishing Limited.
Printed and bound in Great Britain.

Contents

Three Colt Street, Limehouse, *c.* 1906. Local people had a good choice of shops and market stalls along this ancient street, but over the last century the neighbourhood has transformed into an entirely residential one.

Acknowledgements

A book like this gathers strength through the individuals and organisations who have allowed the inclusion of their rare and historic images. In particular, the London Metropolitan Archives (LMA) has kindly allowed the reproduction of pictures from their photographic collections, while Maurice Friedman, Alan A. Jackson, Patricia Hickman, David Brewster and Judges Postcards of Hastings have also made valuable pictorial contributions. Additionally, the expertise of Ray Newton and Steve Kentfield of the History of Wapping Trust has been generously given, while the facilities of Tower Hamlets Local History and Archives, Guildhall Library and LMA have proved invaluable. My sincerest thanks go to all of them. Mention should also be made of those often anonymous photographers whose original work allows us to enjoy once more some fleeting moments from days long past.

Sources

Books consulted include: *London Docklands* by Elizabeth Williamson and Nikolaus Pevsner; *Exploring the East End* by Rosemary Taylor; *The East End Then and Now* by Winston G. Ramsey; *The Hamlets and the Tower* by David Rich; *East End Past* by Richard Tames; *The Isle of Dogs 1066-1918* by Eve Hostettler; *Central Stepney History Walk* by Tom Ridge, and *Aldgate and Stepney Tramways* by Robert J. Hurley.

Introduction

The East End, as defined by the London Borough of Tower Hamlets, is one of the most densely populated parts of the capital and although much of it now has a modern aspect, a century ago it all looked very different. In place of today's great post-war housing estates and up-market river-view apartment blocks were countless neighbourhoods of traditional flat-fronted terraced houses, labyrinthine mazes of tightly packed streets mixed with factories and workshops and where overcrowding and poverty were often part of everyday life.

The neighbourhoods created by London's eastward expansion were as diverse as any in the city, particularly towards the Thames, for here was the Port of London, the world's greatest trading port. Hereabouts life was tied to the river trade and beyond the towering perimeter walls of the great nineteenth-century docks and warehouses, the handling of ship's cargoes ensured the prosperity of the port and the city before containerisation triggered the demise of the old docks.

The ships also brought settlers and immigrants to swell London's population and add flavour to it. Sailors from the Orient settled around Limehouse and raised families, creating the distinctive neighbourhoods of London's first Chinatown. Further north is Spitalfields which became home in the late seventeenth century to French Protestant silk weavers and merchants – their legacy remains in the remarkable neighbourhoods of elegant townhouses which still give a vivid sense of the area's unique history.

Irish and Scandinavian incomers brought their own lifestyles, as did the vast influx of Jews in the nineteenth century – they, like so many others, found London a hospitable city for those driven out of their homelands by oppressive regimes.

This book follows in the footsteps of its predecessor *East Enders' Postcards* and explores some of the neighbourhoods of the former Metropolitan Boroughs of Stepney, Poplar, Bethnal Green and adjacent areas. Once again, postcards form part of the picture source but here it has been enhanced by a selection of the historic images from the collection of the London Metropolitan Archives (LMA) who have been kind enough to allow their inclusion. Also appearing here for the first time is a range of unique photographs from private collections allowing the book to present a fresh pictorial look at one of the most individual and fascinating quarters of the capital city.

Brian Girling
March 2005

one

Maritime
Neighbourhoods

Tower Bridge, *c*. 1906. When first-century Roman invaders began creating the trading settlement of *Londinium* and bridged the great river they knew as *Tamesis* they could not have known they were laying the foundation of the world's greatest trading port. The river was the key to it all and would become a vital commercial highway linking *Londinium* with the heart of the country, the sea and the world. The Roman *Tamesis* bore little resemblance with the fast-flowing Thames we know today; it was wider and shallower with marshy banks, tidal inlets and low islands, one of which provided the bridgehead for the first river crossing, the Roman London Bridge. This was rebuilt many times but the Romans' achievement comes into focus when we realise that it would be a further 1,800 years before another bridge was built on its seaward side. The wait was worth it, for when it came in 1894 the mighty gothic extravaganza that was Tower Bridge was a product of Victorian prosperity and flair for great engineering projects, being a classic alliance of beauty and practicality. Usefully linking neighbourhoods on both sides of the river, the bridge's carriageways could be raised to allow the largest ships passage into the Upper Pool of London and the heart of the city. (Courtesy of Judges Postcards)

Opposite below: The King's (Queen's) House, Tower Green, *c*. 1903. The Tower's roles as prison, royal palace and much more are well known but less familiar are the tiny neighbourhoods within the walls which accommodate the Tower's resident population. There are houses and apartments for Yeoman Warders and Tower officials while the Resident Governor of the Tower of London lives in the house seen here. The King's House was built in around 1540 and once housed high-ranking prisoners including Guy Fawkes and, in 1941, Rudolph Hess. Restoration has since revealed a timbered façade.

The Tower of London from Tower Bridge, *c.* 1894. London's great Norman fortress was begun by William the Conqueror and would play a prominent part in England's turbulent and often bloody history through the second millennium. The new Tower Bridge gave new views of the Tower, one of the earliest of which shows the Thames foreshore still littered with builder's debris.

Tower Bridge looking north, *c.* 1910. The opening of Tower Bridge in 1894 was welcomed by the residents of Bermondsey and Stepney who for the first time could cross the river without a lengthy diversion over London Bridge or through the reeking murk of the Tower subway (1869). Road traffic, much of it comprised of heavy dockland-generated wagons, also welcomed the time saved by the new facility. The photographer has chosen an unusual viewpoint for his shot but in doing so has managed to include the less frequently pictured warehouse complex of St Katharine Docks. The warehouses and the docks they served were built in the 1820s on the site of one of London's more ancient neighbourhoods surrounding the Hospital of St Katharine-by-the-Tower which was founded in 1147. The hospital's fourteenth-century church was lost to the dock building as were many old houses and hovels in streets whose names recalled a rich vein of London history; Pillory Lane, Cat's Hole and Shovel Alley were among them. St Katharine Docks were designed by Thomas Telford and the range of warehouses around the basins by Philip Hardwick, but despite appalling damage during the Second World War the docks did not close until 1968. The closures opened the way for an ambitious redevelopment for St Katharine's which preserved the best of the surviving architecture while opening up the site for public leisure, including a marina in the dock basins and a World Trade Centre (1977), but with a vast concrete hotel to lessen the visual appeal of a highly attractive area.

Opposite above: St Katherine's Way, 1969. Regeneration of the dock area had already begun but dereliction still abounded, corrugated iron hid the dock entrance and the grimy warehouse on St Katherine's Wharf awaited its fate. A new riverside walkway, an hotel and other new facilities would soon transform this old neighbourhood into a smart London showpiece, the first of the old docks to be so treated.

Opposite below: St Katherine's Wharf, 1969. The demise of an old warehouse allows a fresh perspective on a familiar landmark.

Working on the Thames off Wapping, *c.* 1910. The river, with its docks, wharves and associated industries has been a source of livelihood for generations of East Enders living in the historic Thames-side neighbourhoods and communities. (Courtesy of Judges Postcards)

The Glasgow boat, off Wapping, *c.* 1910. Until around seventy years ago it was possible to sail on a passenger ship from the heart of London to a variety of British and continental ports. The twice-weekly service to Glasgow is seen here as it embarks upon its two day voyage, passing St Katharine's Wharf (far left) and the British and Foreign Wharf (centre), where cargoes of wine and spirits filled its warehouses. A surviving landmark is St Katherine Dockmaster's House, dating from 1828.

Hermitage Steam Wharf, Wapping, 1901. A passenger aboard the London & Edinburgh Shipping Co.'s SS *Iona* captured this image of Hermitage Wharf as the vessel drew away en route for Leith, on the east coast of Scotland, a regular service which included cargo as well as passengers.

Hermitage Steam Wharf, *c.* 1920. Barges and lighters crowd around a larger ship as cargo is transferred between the river and the wharf. To the left was the Hermitage Entrance to Hermitage Basin which was built between 1811 and 1821 as an addition to the earlier London Dock (1805), the capital's second oldest enclosed commercial dock. Wapping High Street with Royal Jubilee Buildings (1887) is in the background.

Wapping High Street from Clave Street, *c.* 1918. Wapping was a riverside hamlet whose history can be traced back to Saxon times. It was an area of Thames marshland which frequently flooded until a drainage project in the sixteenth century gave the stabilised ground which allowed the development of Wapping's high street. Maritime trades and activities grew up and, with an abundance of taverns and beerhouses, Wapping evolved into a rip-roaring 'sailor-town' thronged with seamen and home to a variety of nefarious activities including piracy. Life in Wapping's old neighbourhoods changed with the great nineteenth-century dock building schemes which swallowed up entire areas of semi-rural hinterland, but the High Street's narrow course remained constant and became characterised by the lofty walls of its warehouses as London's port prospered. Overhead gangways crisscrossed the roadway and shops were elusive in this most unusual high street. The photograph shows a busy day in the port; heavily laden wagons line the road as cargoes are brought to and taken from the warehouses. To the right are Lower Gun Warehouses while the road runs on towards Wapping Wall where in past centuries an embankment kept the Thames at bay. Despite the twentieth-century exodus downstream of the docks, some of the flavour of these old maritime communities can still be experienced in the midst of the new Wapping and its smart new apartment blocks. Some of these are warehouse conversions and include Prusom's Island, a title which perpetuates a local name for an area of drier ground amid Wapping's ancient marshes.

Above: Wapping from Rotherhithe, *c.* 1908. Congestion was once more of a problem on the river than on the roads – ships sometimes spent days moored in the river waiting for the use of dock facilities. Here is a typically busy river seen against a backdrop of Wapping's Gun Wharves and Paper Wharf by Wapping Dock, home to Jacob Alexander & Co., wastepaper merchants.

Right: Wapping High Street from Brewhouse Lane. It is 1969, the docks have closed but the gentrifiers have yet to arrive. It is a time of decline and decay, but some of the atmosphere of old Wapping remains and the working men's café, run by Mrs Catherine Ciskie on the corner of Brewhouse Lane, is still in business. The bonded warehouses (left) overlooked the site of Execution Dock where, until 1830, river pirates including the notorious Captain Kidd ended their activities on the gallows.

Shadwell Green, *c.* 1918. Apart from some riverside wharves, the hamlet of Shadwell remained relatively undeveloped until the seventeenth century when the arrival of housing and industry transformed the former marshlands into new communities complete with a market house and a pure water supply. By the end of the Victorian era Shadwell was in decline, despite the opening of a successful fish market in 1885. This did not survive long into the twentieth century and the area became home to some of the worst housing in the East End. The photograph records the last of this poor area still to be cleared with the tottering tenements to the right illustrating the wretched state of the neighbourhood. Even where upper floors had become uninhabitable, the ground floors still provided a home of sorts for unfortunate East Enders. Further along towards Gould's Hill sunken windows by the pavement opened into dark damp-plagued subterranean rooms which were a considerable health hazard. The road-surfacing of large boulders would have given a lively ride for anything proceeding at more than walking pace, and the street lamp had long since given up. Fortunately for Shadwell better days lay ahead and, following the death of King Edward VII, it was decided to clear the area of Lower Shadwell and create a much-needed park in memory of the late monarch. Although planned as early as 1910 the park which bore the King's name did not open until 1922 when his son, King George V, performed the opening ceremony. (Courtesy of LMA)

The site of King Edward VII Memorial Park, Lower Shadwell, *c*. 1918. Desolation is all around, the bare earth the former site of grim housing, and the remains of the old riverside fish market are in the distance. Soon grass and trees would provide a new amenity for local people, but one link with the past would remain; a circular building which once provided pedestrian access to the sub-Thames Rotherhithe Tunnel (1904–08). It is still in use for ventilation.

The Thames from Ratcliff Cross Stairs, *c*. 1920. For many East Enders, other than those working in the docks or riverside industries, the Thames was an unseen presence hidden away behind dockland walls and private property. Ratcliff Cross Stairs and other such passages to the Thames gave access to the foreshore and were the haunt of children and 'mud larks'; those who foraged on the shore for a living. Ratcliff Cross Stairs is famed as the embarkation point for sixteenth-century explorer Sir Hugh Willoughby and other navigators who set sail to explore the Arctic seas, their exploits being commemorated by a memorial in Shadwell's park.

Narrow Street from Medland Street and Broad Street (The Highway), Ratcliff, c. 1918. This photograph is from the twentieth century, but with its bow-windowed shops and small narrow houses the scene owes more to the eighteenth century, and is a reminder of how many of these old maritime neighbourhoods looked before the great dock and warehouse developments of the nineteenth century. The picture looks downhill towards the Thames and Ratcliff Cross Stairs before the street turns left and runs close to the river on its way to Limehouse. Regeneration has turned Narrow Street into one of the most desirable addresses in the East End, with many old warehouses tastefully converted into modern homes. A modern development, Keepier Wharf, preserves an old riverside name, while to the left modern St George's Square stands on the site of Messrs Walker, Harrison and Garthwaite's Phoenix Works where ship's biscuits were made. Both Medland Street (left) and Broad Street (right) have been united as The Highway, a thunderous modern traffic artery which descends into the Limehouse Link tunnel close to this spot.

Right: Broad Street by Narrow Street, *c.* 1906. Another look at the commercial Broad Street of a century ago. Coal merchant George Gowland had just vacated his run-down shop and yard, which also fronted the Thames at Keepier Wharf, while boiler-maker Adam Miller remained in business next door. Here also, all the old properties have gone and a modern landmark, Unicorn Building, has taken their sites. (Courtesy of LMA)

Below: Narrow Street looking towards Broad Street, *c.* 1904. More of old maritime Ratcliff with Keepier Wharf behind the fence (left) and an aged nautical pub, The Ship, next door. There is a distant glimpse of Butcher Row beyond the point where a stone cross once stood in Ratcliff's market place. (Courtesy of LMA)

Narrow Street and Ropemakers Fields, Limehouse, *c.* 1902. Limehouse was another of the Thames-side hamlets, its name being derived from the lime-burning kilns or lime houses which from the fourteenth century began to supply building materials for London's houses. A long tradition of shipbuilding began in the sixteenth century, and by the eighteenth century Limehouse, then at London's eastern extremity, was becoming increasingly industrialised, a process accelerated by the opening of Limehouse Cut (canal) in 1770, and Regent's Canal and dock (1820). These gave Limehouse an enviable position as the Thames gateway to the extensive inland waterway network and the area prospered accordingly. The photograph gives a taste of old nautical Limehouse with its bow-windowed ship chandleries and maritime stores, all liberally chalked with the graffiti of the day. To the left at No. 89 Narrow Street were the boarded-up premises of George Morrow, oar, scull and mast-maker with his neighbour James Barnett, ship chandler, at No. 91. There was a wide range of marine supplies to be had here including rope fendoffs (used to fend off a ship's impact with a dock wall or other ships) canvas and ships' lamps – there was also tar and oakum which was used for caulking. Further along in Ropemakers Fields was St Andrews Church Mission and Brasenose Working Men's Club. There was once considerable poverty in this neighbourhood as may be judged by the children in the photograph, two of whom have no shoes. This is in marked contrast to the scene here today with its opulent townhouses facing an open space whose railings incorporate a rope design, a reference to the former local rope-making industry. The name Ropemakers Fields also derives from the local rope-walks which provided rope for anchors and rigging. Ropemakers Fields is now the largest open space in Limehouse. Nightingale Lane (left) became Brightlingsea Place in 1905. (Courtesy of LMA)

Three Colt Street, Limehouse, c. 1902. Three Colt Street winds southwards from Hawksmoor's mighty church of St Anne towards the river and Limekiln Dock. Along the way is Limehouse Causeway, a street whose name recalls an historic route through the Thames marshes. Three Colt Street was once Limehouse's high street and was lined with shops serving the diverse neighbourhoods it passed through. Seen here with a crowd of children outside is Siebert's, the German bakery, with windows piled high with loaves, while next door was Thomas Coates' coffee rooms. His neighbour was David Bruce, gasfitter, a useful service in gas-lit Edwardian London. Also here was a basket-maker, and Charles Wynne, purveyor of that popular East End delicacy, 'Eel and Pie'. In the distance the King's Head pub adorns the Narrow Street corner. These centuries-old weatherboarded properties were among the oldest in the street and were of a type which once abounded in the inner East End – tragically, no examples have survived the twentieth century. The character of Three Colt Street changed as the century progressed and today municipal housing estates rule the roost. Padstow and Bethlehem Houses, part of the Roche Estate, are here now. (Courtesy of LMA)

Number 1 Gate, West India Docks, c. 1906. A statue of dock founder Robert Milligan guards the entrance to this, the first of the great commercial docks, which was built from 1800-05 across the neck of the Isle of Dogs peninsular. Produce from the West Indies was brought here and stored in a vast range of warehouses along the North Quay, once the longest brick building in the world. Seen here is No. 1 Warehouse, now restored and home to the Museum in Docklands (2003).

Millwall, c. 1906. The most distinctive physical feature seen on the map of London is the great meander taken by the Thames as it flows around the Isle of Dogs peninsula. This was once a remote area of Middlesex, much of it lying below the level of the river at high tide. Drainage and embankmenting made the Island suitable for agriculture, but the dock-building of the nineteenth century transformed it as did the shipbuilding yards and other industries which also moved in. New residential communities supplied the workforce and by the middle of the nineteenth century the Island was a thriving and industrious quarter of London. The multiple-view postcard takes a look at Millwall, a community on the western side of the Island – the name deriving from the mills which once drained the marsh. The montage features several neighbourhoods with their Victorian housing, including Strafford Street and Alpha Road (Grove), since rebuilt. At the lower left is Maria Street, once part of old Tooke Town, seen here with its tiny Primitive Methodist Chapel – the towers of the Barkantine Estate (1965-70) are here now. Two views show Millwall's main highway, West Ferry Road, which was laid out in 1812 as the road to the Deptford and Greenwich ferry, and there are pictures of St Luke's church in Strafford Street, which was built from 1868-70 and lost to war damage and later demolition, and the 'Millwall Puffer'. This was the Isle of Dogs' own railway which served the Island from 1871 to the General Strike in 1926, after which it closed.

Opposite below: Union Middle Dock, c. 1895. Union Docks were located between the Upper and Lower Limehouse entrances to West India Docks, an historic site of Thames shipbuilding and repair which continued into the twentieth century with the firm of Fletcher, Son & Fearnall (seen here) who specialised in the building of steam ships. There were dry-dock facilities and a 'gridiron', a beamed construction which supported ships during repair. Part of the old Union Dock site was developed by the Cargo Fleet Iron Co. in the 1930s but it was the 1980s which saw the dramatic transformation of the neighbourhood as the glittering towers of a new city in Docklands, Canary Wharf, arose close by.

Millwall Dock, *c.* 1906. Millwall Dock opened in 1868, its waters taking up a large area at the centre of the Isle of Dogs. The docks handled vast cargoes of grain from the Baltic, and there was a pioneering dry dock. A swing bridge carried West Ferry Road over the dock entrance, but the opening and closing of the bridge to allow shipping through the entrance caused traffic hold-ups, so from 1876 pedestrians had the option of using this elegant cast-iron footbridge. Millwall and West India Docks were linked in 1909 but the whole complex closed in 1980.

Unloading grain in Millwall Docks, *c.* 1930. The scene is overlooked by the mighty Central Granary which was built in 1903 and rose to the height of a thirteen-storey building. Four pneumatic elevators facilitated the unloading of grain into quayside silos.

Manchester Road, Cubitt Town, *c.* 1906. Builder William Cubitt's vision of a new residential and industrial settlement at the tip of the Isle of Dogs slowly took shape through the mid-1800s. There would have been a pioneering spirit among the first Islanders to live in this isolated location before the railway opened in 1871 to give a link with the rest of London. Cubitt's residential terraces were spaciously laid out in tree-lined streets creating a pleasant environment, but war damage and post-war rebuilding saw old neighbourhoods replaced with modern estates. Cubitt's Christ Church (1852) survived the war and is seen here in its original setting with the police station on the right. William Cubitt was Lord Mayor of London in 1860-61.

Manchester Road, Cubitt Town, *c.* 1906. This view, taken near Billson Street, shows the leafy streetscape and bay-windowed houses which characterised Cubitt Town's principal highway.

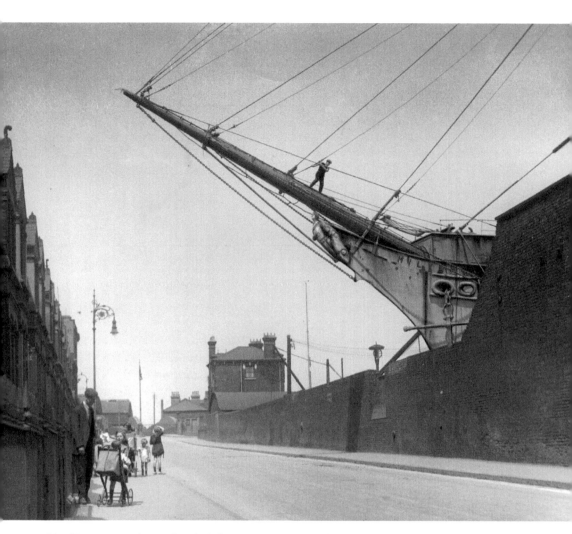

Glen Terrace, Manchester Road, Cubitt Town, *c.* 1919. With the Thames on three of its sides, the waters of the West India Docks on the fourth and the Millwall Docks at its centre, life on the Isle of Dogs was dominated by maritime activities of all kind with nowhere on the Island out of sight or sound of the abundant shipping. Poplar photographer William Whiffen's classic image of Glen Terrace perfectly captures that aspect of Island life as the bowsprit of a vessel under repair in the dock opposite appears to dwarf the houses. The terrace itself was built in the 1890s and the houses were more spacious than usual in Cubitt Town, several of them being the homes of well-to-do local business owners while others were occupied by two or more families. Manchester Road was a busy commercial traffic route at the east of the Island, its quietness here may have been as a result of a 'bridger'; the opening of a swing bridge and closure of the road to allow the passage of a ship.

Opposite below: Off Blackwall, *c.* 1935. Blackwall is famed for its sub-Thames tunnel but it can also boast a maritime heritage from the late sixteenth century when it was a centre for shipbuilding and repair. In later years, the river's principle shipyard was that of Thames Ironworks & Shipbuilding Co. (1846-1912), whose old site can be seen beyond the sailing barge.

The highlights of Edwardian Cubitt Town and Greenwich as pictured on a contemporary postcard. Two of the views show the Island's unexpected beauty spot, Island Gardens, which opened in 1895 giving a fine panorama of the architectural treasures of Greenwich on the opposite bank. Wren's Royal Naval College takes centre stage while the Old Royal Observatory can be seen on the hill behind it.

Blackwall Tunnel, 1895. Despite the Thames's role as a great maritime highway, it was also a considerable barrier for road traffic between communities within sight of one another on the opposite banks. For centuries there was a tortuous journey via London Bridge to cross the river – or a hazardous ferry crossing. Brunel's Thames Tunnel (1843) was to have been the first under-river road east of the City of London, but it opened as a foot-tunnel before railways utilized it from 1869 – it was the world's first tunnel under a navigable river. Londoners had to wait until 1897 for their first road tunnel, the Blackwall, whose construction from 1891 burrowed beneath the old shipbuilding community of Blackwall. The project was one of the newly created London County Council's greatest undertakings and its benefits were immediate. The photograph commemorates an inspection of the as yet unopened tunnel on 30 October 1895 by a gathering which included the Duke of Norfolk (Earl Marshal of England); Lord Rosebery, Prime Minister and first chairman of the LCC and representatives of the building contractors, S. Pearson & Sons. Although designed and built in the age of horse-drawn traffic the tunnel continues to serve London together with a duplicate tunnel opened in 1967.

Thames flood, Orchard Place, Blackwall, January 1928. There were disastrous Thames floods long before there was talk of global warming as freak tides and North Sea storm surges swamped the low-lying riversides. Some East Enders may remember the inundations of 1928 when a tide which was eighteen inches above the highest recorded in over a century swept into vulnerable neighbourhoods drowning them in polluted water – the Thames was a dirty river in 1928. Located between the rivers Lea and Thames, Orchard Place was at considerable risk, and as the water rose in the darkness of night, terrified residents clambered upstairs, some in their nightclothes, to await rescue which, for some, did not come until the next morning.

The rescuers and the rescued, Orchard Place.

Thames flood, Orchard Place, January 1928. Despite an ebbing tide, much floodwater remained trapped in the streets with a boat the only means of bringing warm clothing, fuel and eventual rescue for those still marooned upstairs. Here one lady makes a nerve-wracking descent into a heavily loaded rowing boat from the balcony of a pub. Central London also suffered in the floods as the monstrous tide swept upstream drowning several residents of basement rooms in Millbank.

two

Traders' Places

Wentworth Street from Petticoat Lane market, *c.* 1900. The East End is reputed to have more markets than anywhere else in Europe and on a Sunday morning when the streets from Aldgate to Bethnal Green are thronged with bargain hunters that fact is evident. With a history spanning four centuries, Petticoat Lane is the most renowned of them and is famed far beyond the East End. Its earliest days saw ladies' garments being sold here, which is the probable origin of the name, but in around 1830 the street was renamed Middlesex Street, this being the boundary of that county and the City of London. The Lane and its environs became home to eighteenth-century Huguenot silk weavers and in the nineteenth century the old neighbourhoods were settled by Jewish immigrants who created the largest Jewish community outside mainland Europe. While Petticoat Lane remains a Sunday market, Wentworth Street trades on weekdays with a wide choice of domestic and clothing stalls. The photograph looks back to the market during its Jewish phase capturing a typical moment as a pair of stallholders point out the delights of their stock to a prospective shopper, who appears unimpressed by the display of fish exposed to the full glare of the sun. In the background is Joseph Israel's grocery shop on the corner of Corea Place, a tiny side turning which would soon disappear in a rebuilding scheme.

Opposite below: Short Street (Leyden Street), *c.* 1906. Petticoat Lane has many tributaries including this side street where costermongers and general dealers traded from barrows rather than stalls. Jewish poulterers had a considerable presence here – their chickens were killed and plucked in the street, a common sight hereabouts. Crates of live chickens can be seen by the barrows. (Courtesy of Maurice Friedman)

Petticoat Lane market, 1935. The Lane was as busy as ever in the 1930s although the type of merchandise on offer had changed through the decades. Here an informal snapshot pictures an alluring display of gentlemen's braces while beyond is a branch of Monnickendam's, the caterers, where a weary shopper could seek coffee and, reputedly, the finest cakes and pastries in the East End. Note the police public call post.

Hare Street (Cheshire Street) from Brick Lane and Sclater Street, *c.* 1910. With its beigel shops and synagogues Brick Lane traversed the heartland of the old Jewish East End on its long run from Whitechapel to Bethnal Green Road. Here were more specialist markets including Sclater Street's bird market – Londoners were introduced to bird keeping by Huguenot immigrants in the eighteenth century. A pair of bird-dealers' shops with their cages can be seen in the photograph.

Club Row bicycle market, Bethnal Green Road, *c.* 1910. This was the place to buy a cut-price machine but with a proliferation of stolen bicycles on offer the 'bargain' was not always what it seemed. Violent scenes were commonplace as an original owner spotted an errant machine, and the police were never far away.

Dog market, Club Row, Bethnal Green Road, *c.* 1895. The junction with Bethnal Green Road and Sclater Street was once the scene of a raucous animal market as buyers and sellers of man's best friend gathered to do business on a Sunday morning.

A rat seller in the dog market, *c.* 1895. This gentleman would have catered for a thoroughly disreputable side of the Victorian canine trade, supplying rats which were used as live bait in dog-fighting contests. This 'sport' was conducted in animal fighting pits at local pubs in the days before such activities became outlawed.

White Lion Street (Folgate Street) from Norton Folgate, *c.* 1906. What is now a mostly residential street was, a century ago, home to a diverse assortment of traders housed in one of Spitalfields' historic terraces. The corner shop on the right was occupied by Hope Bros, the hosiers, while furrier Morris Mizel had set up next door at No. 2. Tailor Henry Jordan was his neighbour and No. 6 was occupied by Elizabeth Morgan's City Dairy where cows were kept in a yard at the back. A builder and another furrier traded from Nos 8 and 10, with Philip Epstein, cap-maker, at No. 12. There was a chandler's shop next door while No. 16 housed B. Schönwetter, a wholesale human hair merchant. Somers & Co. cigar merchants, traded from No. 18, a fine old house which, like its fellows at the far end of the terrace, dated from the 1720s. This house was destined to become one of the most remarkable in London following its acquisition by American Denis Severs who set about a meticulous recreation of the house's original form as a Huguenot merchant's townhouse. It is now No. 18 Folgate Street – the street was renamed in 1939. White Lion Street evolved out of White Lion Yard which in the seventeenth century was a cul-de-sac off Norton Folgate, the northern continuation of Bishopsgate. This Spitalfields neighbourhood was taking shape as a new suburb of the City of London, and as smart terraces of townhouses arose, the area became a focus for Huguenot settlers from France who were making London their new home.

Opposite above: Salmon Lane, Limehouse, *c.* 1906. This was typical of the small neighbourhood markets which, with their accompanying shops, supplied the everyday needs of communities throughout the East End. Salmon Lane's branch of the popular Home & Colonial Stores enhanced the facilities together with a beer shop (right) and the Copenhagen pub in the distance. There was also a pawn shop for when times were hard.

Opposite below: Roman Road by Usher Road, Old Ford, *c.* 1906. The name denotes the road's origins but 'The Roman' market came much later in the mid-1800s. Here, the flower sellers have set out a colourful display and a century on much of the market's traditional appeal remains. (Courtesy of Patricia Hickman)

A front-room shop, Bethnal Green, *c.* 1920. Shops in the East End ranged from the departmental grandeur of Wickham's ('the Harrods of the East') to modest premises like this where householders traded from their front rooms. Enamel advertisements nailed to the shutters recall once-familiar products while a poster highlights forthcoming attractions at the Museum cinema, Cambridge (Heath) Road.

Red Lion Street by Watts Street, Wapping, *c.* 1928. Back street shops like these drew their customers from tiny catchment areas, but in these populous neighbourhoods there was no shortage of business. Confectioner Esther Fairclough's shop (left) kept the locals supplied with sweets and tobacco while further along were the emporia of James Insole, grocer, and John Wilson, butcher. The milk cart on its rounds had come from Richard Lewis's Hermitage Dairy in nearby Hermitage Street. Red Lion Street in 1928 was a relic of old Wapping which had survived the massive construction works for London Dock (1805) and its warehousing. Part of the street was once known as Anchor & Hope Alley – a partly obliterated street nameplate was still in place on the single house. The photograph records the last of this old community with the imminent closure of the shops followed by clearance of all the buildings to make way for the London County Council's Wapping Estate. The flats of Beechey House (1929) are by this corner now and the street was renamed Reardon Path in 1939. (Courtesy of LMA)

Opposite below: A barber shop, No. 138 East India Dock Road, Poplar. A neighbourhood barber makes good use of his front room. Here the local pleasure palace was the Queens Theatre in Poplar High Street – a poster gives details of the Thursday matinee. (Courtesy of Maurice Friedman)

Butcher shop, No. 159 White Horse Street, Stepney, *c.* 1905. Looking every inch the successful Edwardian shopkeeper, butcher Joseph Samson Peatling poses with his wife outside their premises which were the last of the small shops in White Horse Street (now White Horse Road) before Ben Jonson Road. Since around 1904 when they took over the shop, the Peatlings had invested a great deal of pride in their business, an aspect of their trading which comes over well in this photograph by Cambridge Studio of Mile End. The spectacularly carnal display has been carefully set out and was typical of such shops in Victorian and Edwardian times – and judging by the pristine state of the butcher's aprons, the day's work had yet to begin. Such shops were a fine amenity for the neighbourhoods they served and the popularity of this one ensured its survival as a family business until the Second World War. Although these shops have long gone there is still a wonderful flavour of the old neighbourhood close by in Durham Row with a rare terrace of original houses. Modern Pevensey House has taken the place of the shops in Ben Jonson Road, whose backs are seen on the right.

Above: A staff group at John Bull's butcher shop, No. 292 Roman Road, Old Ford, 1911. The postcard was written by 'Emily' (far right) to her friend Pollie Last in Bethnal Green to tell her that she was leaving her job at the shop.

Right: Walter Daniel, timber merchant, Abbey Street (Buckfast Street), Bethnal Green, *c*. 1920. This business specialised in wood for rustic garden work, tree stakes and toy making, and was accommodated in what had once been a silk weaver's house. The long top windows had been designed to allow the maximum daylight into the weaver's rooms thereby extending the working day. The timber trade did not need so much daylight but the windows made useful advertising space.

Above: William Sutton & Sons, milliners, Bethnal Green Road, *c.* 1920. The elaborate confections on offer here would have tempted the local ladies at a time when it would have been unthinkable to have gone out of doors without a hat.

Left: Shop at No. 468 Commercial Road East, Stepney, *c.* 1913. Tobacconist and confectioner Simon Weitzman and his family had just taken over this traditional shop from previous owners the Wilson brothers. It was part of a row of small shops running between Bower Street and Stepney Causeway and known as Upton Terrace. A newspaper's placard 'Mrs Pankhurst and the bomb' refers to an incident in the ongoing Suffragette campaign. There are new neighbourhoods here now, part of the Pitsea Estate.

Above: Wellclose Square (west side), Stepney, *c.* 1920. The eighteenth-century houses were once the abode of the wealthy, but as workshops and other commercial interests moved in, the crash of iron-shod wheels on stone setts and the shouts of the carmen banished the tranquility of old for a diminishing band of residents.

Right: An East End fish shop, No. 413 Commercial Road East, *c.* 1908. With its eye-catching display of locally cured and dried fish, Thomas Cambridge's business was typical of the area, but its open front left everything exposed to the dust of a busy main road.

'The Little Wonder', Rhodeswell Road, Limehouse, 1912. This narrow street winds its way through northern Limehouse, closely following the course of the Regent's canal, and was once lined with tiny houses and neighbourhood shops of which this was a typical example. Arthur Moates' newspaper shop was located between Tye Street and Salmon Lane and had all but disappeared under a surfeit of advertising and newspaper placards trumpeting the headlines of the day. It was 1912 and a dramatic news story had broken earlier in the year with the loss of the White Star liner RMS *Titanic* on her maiden voyage. Although the great maritime tragedy had ceased to make the headlines, an illustrated periodical in the window display retold the story of that awful night. The *Daily Mirror's* placard promised photographs of the latest wonder, flying machines – aviation was then in its infancy. Other placards reveal some lost titles; *Daily Chronicle*, *Morning Leader* and *Daily Sketch*, all at one halfpenny a time, while other publications had colourful posters for their latest fictional stories. To the left of the shop was Walter Stanley's hairdressing saloon in what had previously been Mrs Emma Hunter's eel pie shop.

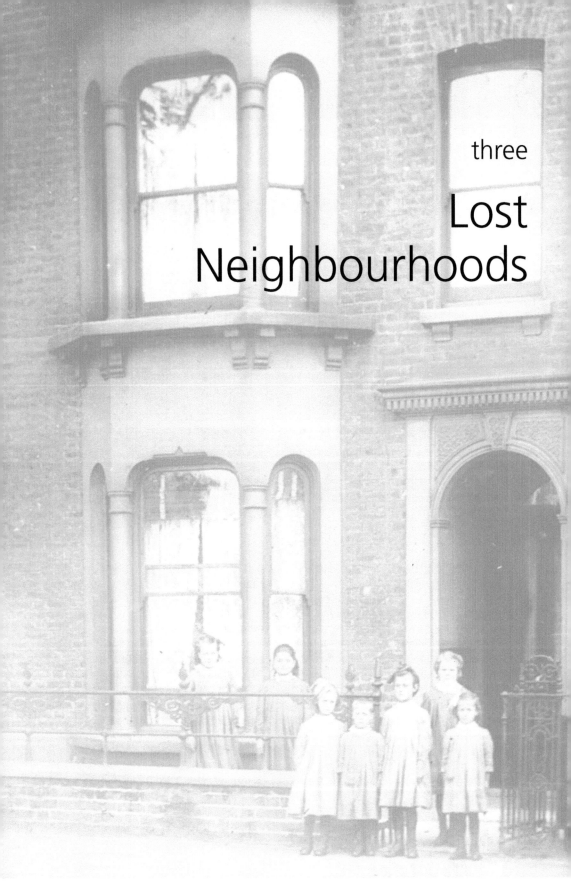

three

Lost
Neighbourhoods

Medland Street (The Highway), Limehouse, c. 1904. The East End entered the twentieth century with much of its housing stock in poor condition and ripe for replacement. The LCC and local authorities had made a start but the devastation of two world wars accelerated the need for rebuilding on a vast scale, leading to the rise of the great municipal housing estates we know today. Increasing road usage was bringing its own problems in thoroughfares like Medland Street, seen here, where the narrowness of the road was such that only a single wagon could pass by. This was impractical in a busy dockland road but here at least a widening scheme was about to transform the neighbourhood in another of the LCC's early projects. The whole of the row on the right in the photograph was ready for demolition, and the LCC were advertising a sale of fixtures and fittings in what had been part of Joseph White's brass foundry. Apart from a chandler's shop, the rest of the row had been residential up to London Street, which can be spotted by a distant wagon delivering lamp oil. The Rainbow pub on the left survived the rebuilding but it went in the end, leaving nothing here today to remind us of this classic East End neighbourhood. Part of old London Street has been renamed Spert Street while everywhere are the exclusive apartment blocks of newly fashionable Docklands with the roaring mouth of the Limehouse Link tunnel close by. (Courtesy of LMA)

Above: Leman Street from Little Alie Street, Whitechapel, *c.* 1900. Many neighbourhoods were populated by former immigrants who had set up homes and businesses in London. Part of the capital's German community was based around Leman Street where German-speaking shopkeepers and publicans attended to the needs of exiles who were, perhaps, nostalgic for their homelands. There would have been plentiful good cheer at Otto Damm's White Hart pub, the fourth building in this row.

Right: Aldgate Hotel, Aldgate High Street, *c.* 1905. Joseph Well's Münchener Bierhalle and Restaurant was a good meeting point for Whitechapel's German community, where Münchener Löwenbrau available at 2d and 4d a glass for the local lager drinkers. The Rose and Crown next door catered for more traditional tastes.

Queen Street, Tower Hill, 1900. The newly opened Tower Bridge had generated so much additional traffic that a whole neighbourhood south of Royal Mint Street had to be cleared for more road space. Included were King and Queen Streets, an historic and picturesque enclave of shopkeepers living within a stone's throw of the Tower of London. (Courtesy of LMA)

Royal Mint Street from Sparrow Corner, Minories, 1900. These old buildings were once part of semi-rural Rosemary Lane but their long lives were about to end with the clearances for the Tower Bridge approach road scheme. There was time for a final sale at Tidmarsh and Brown's china shop, but builder Samuel Blow had already left the historic No. 3½ next door. The Royal Mint had moved from the Tower of London in 1810 but it took another forty years for Rosemary Lane to be renamed. (Courtesy of LMA)

Upper East Smithfield and St George Street (The Highway), *c.* 1917. The towering perimeter walls of London Docks overlook a street busy with heavy commercial traffic which was still being drawn by horse. A lost neighbourhood to the left included Well Street (with the wall posters), now called Ensign Street, while the now considerably widened main road is part of The Highway, a major route to the east from the City.

Wellclose Square, Stepney, *c.* 1920. The great days of Wellclose Square were over. The elegant enclave where ship's captains and Scandinavian timber merchants had once made their homes now housed John White's Seamen's Boarding House (centre) where the visiting sailor could seek a cheap berth for the night. To its left is Grace's Alley and Wilton's Music Hall (1850s) which is being restored.

South side of Wellclose Square, by Neptune Street, *c.* 1920. With the Danish church (1696) which once stood at its centre, and the Prince of Denmark pub (later Wilton's) close by, this was a partly Scandinavian area before its Jewish population expanded in the 1800s with the arrival of a synagogue and the Jewish almshouses on the square's southern side.

Red Lion Street from Tench Street, Wapping, 1904. The narrow teeming streets of the Wapping of a century ago were typified by this populous byway which had formerly been called Anchor & Hope Alley. Further along the street once stood an alehouse where local tradition has it that the fleeing Judge Jeffreys of the notorious Bloody Assize was captured in 1688. The street behind the camera was once called Broad Street (now Reardon Street) where Captain William Bligh of 'Mutiny on the Bounty' fame once lived. These old neighbourhoods were swept away in the 1920s to make way for the LCC's Wapping Estate. (Courtesy of LMA)

Opposite below: North side of Wellclose Square, by Shorter Street, *c.* 1920. The photograph shows the square overwhelmed by carmen and carriers while a distant terrace offers a reminder of past glories. Decades of neglect and decay culminated in the destruction in the 1960s of what should have been an architectural treasure in the East End.

Red Lion Street, Wapping, *c.* 1929. The sad spectacle of an East End neighbourhood in its last days, with the de-licensed pub, the Old George, slowly decaying in the rain. (Courtesy of LMA)

Raymond Street by Watts Street, Wapping, *c.* 1929. Raymond Street ran parallel with Red Lion Street and suffered a similar fate with its clearance for the Wapping Estate. In these congested narrow streets there was only room for a wall-chalked goal for the young footballers of the neighbourhood. (Courtesy of LMA)

Back Church Lane by Fairclough Street, Whitechapel, *c.* 1909. Furniture dealer Isaac Alterson had just vacated his corner shop and the other houses were shuttered in readiness for demolition which would provide a site for a new LCC school in 1910. To the left was some redundant stabling formerly used by the London General Omnibus Co. in that era of horse-drawn buses. (Courtesy of LMA)

Fairclough Street, Whitechapel, *c.* 1909. This early nineteenth-century byway was named North Street when it was first built, but a change was made to lessen the duplication of a common street name. A few neighbours had gathered by their doors, but the houses had reached the end of their lives although Myer Rattman's general store on the Berner (now Henriques) Street corner was still in business. (Courtesy of LMA)

Matilda Street, Commercial Road, *c.* 1937. Older parts of the East End were often made up of a maze of back streets, alleys and courts with tiny houses and commercial premises utilising every inch of space. The neighbourhoods bisected by Commercial Road were particularly densely populated and labyrinthine in character. Matilda Street (Christian Place from 1939) was a tiny cul-de-sac off Christian Street and connected to Grove Street (later Golding Street) by a tunnel-like passage seen here in the background. Remarkably, Matilda Street had an even smaller side turning – Matilda Place – with just four houses. Despite its diminutive size, Matilda Street was a busy place with three shops including those of Simon Scoop; butcher, and Abraham Lewis; greengrocer whose very basic premises are seen with the stock, including a pail full of firewood spilling out onto the pavement. There was also an engineering works and, in this Jewish neighbourhood, the tiny Matilda Street synagogue. Although no one had much living space, these back courts and alleys made a safe playground for local children and a watchful neighbour was usually close by. There is nothing today to indicate that Matilda Street had ever existed – the modern Berner Estate is here now and Christian Street has been entirely rebuilt, as has Golding Street. (Courtesy of LMA)

Umberston Street, Commercial Road, *c.* 1938. These lengthy terraces were built as residential Marman Street, but in a populous neighbourhood many of the cottages doubled as 'front room' shops. Jacobs Mansions (left) was a later addition, and has survived the post-war demise of the older properties and their replacement with small business units. The radio shop on the left was popular in an age when few could afford the latest luxury, television. (Courtesy of LMA)

Walburgh Street from Upper Chapman Street, Stepney, *c.* 1900. There was a mixture of workshops and small houses on the site of the modern Bigland housing estate. A building on the corner of Lower Chapman Street (now Bigland Street) is a lone survivor. (Courtesy of LMA)

Watney Street, Shadwell, 1977. The picture gives a glimpse of an old East End neighbourhood in transition as worn out and war-damaged properties linger on for a while longer and empty sites are the result of piecemeal clearance. Behind the camera is a smart new Watney Market which had just replaced one of the East End's busiest street markets, but to the left are two examples of war-damaged buildings which had been sufficiently patched up to allow the shops to continue. Here are Joseph Smith – 'Joe the Grocer' – a longstanding Watney Street trader, and neighbouring butcher Simon Press on the Sheridan Street corner. A derelict stretch leads on to Brinsley Street and the Anchor & Hope pub – also Martha Street and the Lord Nelson pub. The railway bridge is by Shadwell station (the Docklands Light Railway would arrive here in 1987) and beyond it there is still a classic East End neighbourhood with small houses, shops and a tiny pub. To the right of the picture all the old shops have been cleared away including butcher A.G. Hedges' former premises on the Dunch Street corner. An early post-war housing scheme by Stepney Council provided the Tarling Estate, one of whose blocks (since demolished) can be seen top left. (Courtesy of Alan A. Jackson)

Opposite above: St George Street (The Highway), *c.* 1895. In a previous incarnation as Ratcliff Highway, the street was as notorious as any in London following a series of murders in 1811. In Victorian times St George Street was raucous with sailor's taverns and Irish pubs while curious sounds were liable to emerge from Jamrach's Menagerie where wild animals were bought and sold. This view looking eastward includes the Prince Regent pub (right) and the distant Artichoke by Artichoke Hill.

Opposite below: Cable Street by Solander Street, *c.* 1938. Populous communities abounded along lengthy Cable Street, this being a typical example. Abraham Rosenberg's corner shop kept the locals supplied with the products of the day while shoe repairer Michael Finkleson (right) kept the neighbourhood well shod. Solander Street and the housing estate which replaced it were named after botanist Daniel Solander (1736-82). (Courtesy of LMA)

Three Colt Street, Limehouse, *c.* 1923. These old properties, located between Grenade Street and Limehouse Causeway, were first seen in the Edwardian photographs on pages 6 and 23 but here, some twenty years on, they are crumbling into terminal dereliction. There were once five of these weatherboarded survivals but two had already gone, opening up a view of Whitehall Place, right, which was previously reached through a dark, tunnel-like passage. Its surviving wooden wall is seen by the prop which is holding the building up. Despite its desperate condition, one of these venerable relics continued to provide an income for E. Bond & Sons, carmen and haulage contractors, while a greengrocery occupied the shop and a ramshackle collection of barrels, crates and a pram which served as a street market stall. The other two shops had already been vacated by Joseph Rawling, who ran a coffee shop and German baker John Siebert who had traded through several decades in this street. (Courtesy of LMA)

Opposite below: Pennyfields, Limehouse, *c.* 1955. As Chinatown's property slowly decayed, old oriental businesses gradually moved away, but in the mid-1950s there was still a Chinese presence. Here, Ching's Restaurant and neighbouring butcher Fong Kow are still in business, while elsewhere in the street the Chinese Seamen's Club, a Chinese lodging house and the Chun Yee Chinese Society remained active. By the mid-1960s the Chinese businesses had dwindled away. (Courtesy of LMA)

Chinese Mission House, No. 92 West India Dock Road, Limehouse, *c.* 1900. Limehouse was noted for its Anglo-Chinese neighbourhoods centred around Pennyfields and Limehouse Causeway. These communities sprung from the oriental seamen who settled here in the mid-1800s, their descendants remaining in Limehouse until post-war rebuilding caused their numbers to decline. The Chinese Mission House had a long spell of Chinese occupancy – it ended its days in the 1960s as the Pekin Restaurant.

Commercial Road Bridge, Limehouse, *c.* 1906. Commercial Road opened in 1804 to speed road traffic between West India Docks and the City of London. In Limehouse the road also served the industries beside the Regent's Canal which it crosses here beside a pair of factories making galvanized iron (right). Buildings on the left included a ship's biscuit-making factory and several metal dealers, all backing onto Regent's Canal Dock. The distant tower belonged to St Matthew's church which, following war damage, was replaced by the Limehouse Christian Centre.

East India Dock Road, Poplar, *c.* 1906. The landmark George Green School (1883), now Tower Hamlets College, still graces the street having survived the demise and rebuilding of its surrounding neighbourhoods.

Burdett Road by Pixley Street, Limehouse, *c.* 1908. These tall houses represented a more 'up-market' neighbourhood along a road which opened in 1862 as a route between Mile End and the docks, crossing Bow Common. The houses on the left have survived but on the right the modernity of multi-storey Butler House on the Burdett housing estate has replaced the old terraces.

Burdett Road between Bridge Street and Bow Common Lane, *c.* 1906. In Edwardian days there was a horse-drawn tram service, plentiful shops and a useful street market for this populous neighbourhood which grew up in the 1860s and 1870s. The popular Nonconformist East London Tabernacle is visible in the distance with Mile End Road on the horizon.

Knott Street from Masters Street, Mile End, *c.* 1937. The high viewpoint of a typical East End neighbourhood allows a glimpse into the usually hidden world behind the houses. These homes were products of the early 1800s, lowly in character and displaying the standard flat-fronted East End style at the front but with a selection of variations at the back including some houses which had no rear upstairs room. The tiny backyards had the usual clutter of such places and featured pantiled washhouses and privies which were often shared by more than one family. The portable zinc bathtub was stored outside and brought inside for the weekly bathe – the water was heated in a copper, and the same water was sometimes used by the whole family. With no indoor toilets, chamber pots were an essential for those who did not relish a night-time visit to the outdoor privy. The view looks towards distant Cadiz Street and was to have been a last look at this old community following its acquisition by the LCC for slum clearance and re-housing, but the war intervened and held up further progression. By 1941 almost everything seen here was a bombsite, but after the war the work of creating the vast Ocean Estate resumed with the massive Bengal House taking up the old Knott Street site. (Courtesy of LMA)

Opposite below: Shandy Street from Duckett Street, (Ocean Estate), *c.* 1937. Originally called Alfred Street, Shandy Street displayed the local characteristic, extremely lengthy terraces of plain-fronted houses. The rows were broken on the right by St Faith's church and its parish hall (1891), the latter being all that has survived. The street now traverses the heartland of the Ocean Estate with the 1940s-built Anson House in place of the houses on the left. (Courtesy of LMA)

Ocean Street from Masters Street, *c.* 1937. The camera has swung round to show more of Ocean Street with its corner shop and the taller houses of Trafalgar Square lying beyond. Trafalgar Square was one of four places in London with this famous name – this particular road is now Trafalgar Gardens. Development of the Ocean Estate began in 1939 – it would eventually swallow up everything seen here. (Courtesy of LMA)

Ely Terrace, *c.* 1938. This was a one-sided street, its single terrace stretching for a prodigious length along what was, in its rural past, a footpath from Mile End to Bow. Floristan and other side streets ran up to Mile End Road, part of a dense network of streets which were eventually lost to the Ocean Estate. (Courtesy of LMA)

XX Place, Globe Town, 1953. In a city as vast and diverse as London it is not surprising that amongst its streets are some whose names are distinctly odd. One of the most curious was XX Place, the only street in London whose name commenced with the alphabet's antepenultimate letter. The street itself was much less remarkable, just a single row of nineteenth-century cottages in a cul-de-sac off Globe Road, to the rear of Stepney Green Underground station. Midway along the terrace one house stood proud of its fellows by the thickness of a single brick. This was once an alehouse, its upper storey containing a plaque with a representation of a barrel and the letters 'XX' denoting 'ale of medium strength and quality'. It is possible that the cottages acquired their name through familiarity with the plaque if no other identification was displayed. XX Place is seen here in 1953, coronation year, with each house adorned with a portrait of the Queen by its patriotic householders – but the end was close for the old houses, and with them went their unique name. (Courtesy of LMA)

Opposite below. Edwards Road, Mile End, *c.* 1906. A lost 1870s-built street tucked away between Burdett Road and Eric Street with the back of the East London Tabernacle just off-camera to the left. The housing now is made up of the medium-rise blocks of the Eric Estate.

Roman Road by Grove Road, *c.* 1906. This was once a rural road called the Driftway with a turnpike where it crossed Grove Road. Victorian London swallowed it up and built St Barnabas church (1865) – its spire would be lost to war damage. The Earl of Aberdeen pub (right) boasted an impressive lighting display which would have shone brightly in the gas-lit street. The area has since gone full circle and reverted to its original greenery with the creation of post-war Mile End Park, here called Haverfield Green – it extends northwards towards Victoria Park.

Underwood Street and Vallance Road, Mile End, 1913. Another East End neighbourhood in its final days as the demolition men move in to clear the site for a new school. A. Gold's corner shop had served its last customer but the walls still display a mass of posters which detail the local entertainment options. These include a 'Ragtime Operette and Carnival' at the Mile End Empire; a variety show at the Cambridge, Commercial Street and for those with a taste for cinema there were 'animated pictures' at the Pavilion Theatre in Whitechapel Road. In this Jewish quarter many of the posters were printed in Yiddish. (Courtesy of LMA)

Anglesea Street, Vallance Road, c. 1950. The railway arches endure, but an attractive small housing estate called Fakruddin Street has replaced this old Jewish neighbourhood.

High Street, Bow (Bromley High Street), *c.* 1928. Medieval Bow was the last place in Middlesex on the great London to Colchester highway before the road crossed the river Lea at Bow Bridge and into Essex. In the 1920s there were still corners of Bow and Bromley in which something of the atmosphere of an East Anglian village lingered with weatherboarded and pantiled cottages, even though London's rapidly expanding suburbs had long since caught up with and absorbed the old settlements. The postcard pictures a tranquil scene in the High Street with an ancient whitewashed cottage (far left) which housed florist Mrs Sarah Harniman, while next door boot repairer Henry George traded from tiny gabled premises which dated from the seventeenth century. The postcard was purchased from his neighbour, tobacconist Mrs Emma Ayton – the writer of the card describes her shop as being 'over 200 years old'. Opposite, and on the Bow Road corner, was the Black Swan pub which had been rebuilt following its destruction in one of London's first ever wartime air raids in 1916. The rebuilt pub did not survive for long – part of the vast Bow Bridge housing estate is here now. Two elements of the picture have survived; Our Lady and St Catherine's Catholic church (1870), and the statue of Prime Minister William Gladstone (1882) which still gazes Londonwards.

Malmesbury Road, Bow, c. 1905. Rows of terraced houses like these made up much of London's housing stock as the Victorian city expanded into the countryside. In Bow the local builders added a touch of individuality to the houses with round-headed windows.

Addington Road, Bow, c. 1905. This street was built for more well-to-do Victorians, and included an impressive detached house, Shaftesbury Villa, on the right. The houses backed onto the Great Eastern Railway's Bow Road station which opened in 1892 and lasted until 1949.

Left: At home in Caxton Street (now Caxton Grove), Bow, *c.* 1906. This large family would have made for a lively household (the writer of this postcard called it 'The Menagerie'), but the house and those in the two preceding photographs have all gone in favour of Tower Hamlets' post-war Malmesbury East Estate.

Below: Tredegar Road, Bow, *c.* 1908. The attractiveness of the street has not prevented rebuilding with modern housing; Stayers House now stands by Balmer Street (right) and Berebinder House by St Stephens Road (left). This name recalls Bearbinder Lane, a former name of Tredegar Road from the days when it ran through fields to the hamlet of Old Ford. The postcard was sent by a resident who laments the return from a holiday in Great Yarmouth to 'wretched and dull' Bow.

Donald Street from Devas Street, Bromley, 1904. These grim houses just survived into the twentieth century but they were already condemned as part of the LCC's Favonia Street clearance scheme, which in part provided a new children's playground. Meanwhile, the neighbourhood's plentiful youngsters had to create what amusement they could from the muddy street – the arrival of the photographer of this picture would have made a welcome diversion and an insistence to be in the photograph. For all its poverty, Donald Street once had a pair of chandler's shops but their stock would have been meagre; just household essentials such as candles, firewood and possibly lamp oil. The tall building in the background provides a link with the present day; it is St Andrew's Hospital (1871) which still stands; but the view today is profoundly different with the Blackwall Tunnel Approach Road thundering away to the right and a new link road, Twelvetrees Crescent, complete with some landscaping on the site of old houses. (Courtesy of LMA)

Old Ford Road by Appian Road, Old Ford, *c.* 1906. This road originated as a rural highway linking Bethnal Green, Globe Town and Old Ford, the latter's name being derived from a Roman crossing of the river Lea. Of the side streets and houses in this Edwardian view, the only survivals are the shops on the right and a former Wesleyan chapel. To the left was Appian Road with Alfred Fennell's domestic stores on the corner – Henry Gadd's fried-fish shop was at the far left.

Evesham Houses, Old Ford Road, Bethnal Green, *c.* 1906. Not everywhere in the East End has changed beyond recognition – this stretch of road still looks much as it did a century ago.

Above and below: Grimsby Street, Brick Lane, Bethnal Green, *c.* 1950. This grimy byway, sandwiched between the Great Eastern Railway viaduct and the shops of Hare Street (Cheshire Street), was called St John Street until 1909. With the constant smoke and smuts from the steam trains this was not the most agreeable place to live but it was convenient for the workshops also located here. Grimsby Street looked particularly grim in these post-war pictures but by the 1990s, and with the old tenements rebuilt, the area began to acquire the gritty appeal of an old East End neighbourhood made good as the colourful ethnic trendiness of Brick Lane gradually permeated its side streets.

Shepherd's Place arch and Tenter Street from White's Row, Spitalfields, *c.* 1909. The earliest residential streets in Spitalfields date from the early 1700s, but it was not until the 1820s that the last of them, Tenter Street, was laid out on the Tenter Grounds, an area once used for stretching and drying cloth in the open air. The archway built in 1810 led into this rather Dickensian neighbourhood with its Jewish shopkeepers, tenement housing and long-vanished Freeman, Palmer and Tilley Streets. Much of the area was lost in the 1920s for the building of the LCC's Holland Estate. (Courtesy of LMA)

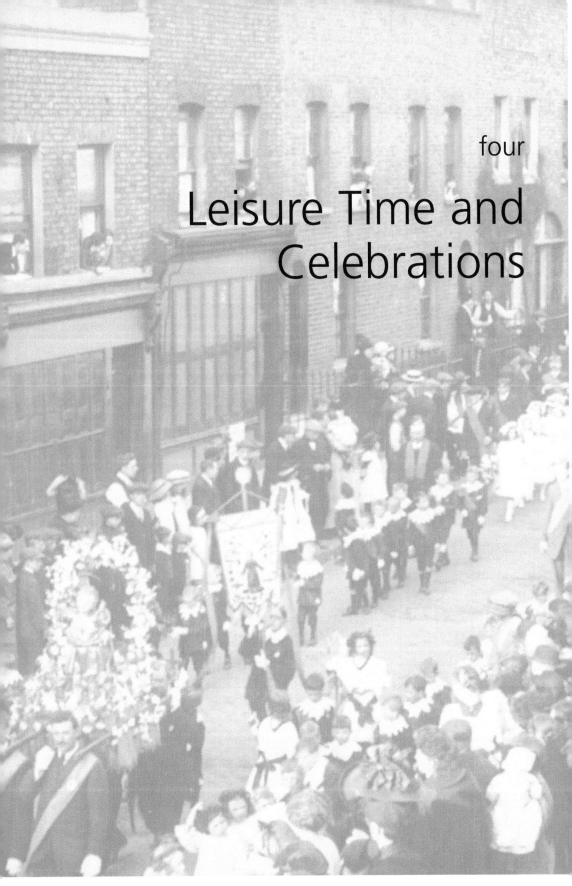

four

Leisure Time and Celebrations

Queen Victoria's Diamond Jubilee Military Parade, Mile End Road, 19 June 1897. Patriotic East Enders will celebrate a Royal event with an enthusiasm rarely matched elsewhere, particularly when the area is touched by some of the capital's legendary pageantry. When Queen Victoria celebrated her Diamond Jubilee, London and the East End were treated to a colourful military parade which, as one observer put it was 'a military display which has not been equaled within the memory of the oldest inhabitant'. The procession with its mounted Lifeguards' band is seen as it passed the People's Palace, a cultural and leisure centre which the Queen had opened ten years earlier in her Golden Jubilee year. The People's Palace entered into the Jubilee spirit with a re-enactment of Victoria's Coronation in 1837 and there was an act of Thanksgiving on the Sunday of Jubilee week. Although there were no formal street decorations, the roads were vivid with householders' and shopkeepers' displays, although it was noted that Commercial Road was sparsely adorned.

Opposite: Jubilee decorations at the Queen beerhouse, Rhodeswell Road, Limehouse, 1897. This modest but appropriately named establishment showed its patriotism with a colourful display, the royal 'VR' being made up of coloured lamps. (Courtesy of Maurice Friedman)

Royal Canadian Mounted Police in West Ferry Road, by Strafford Street, Isle of Dogs, June 1911. A colourful spectacle for Islanders as a contingent of eighty 'Mounties' march to Chelsea Barracks in readiness to play their part in the Coronation of King George V. Having disembarked at Millwall they are seen passing St Luke's School.

After the Royal Visit, Mile End Road, 25 May 1935. As part of their Silver Jubilee celebrations, George V and Queen Mary drove through the East End in an open landau to the delight of so many East Enders, some fainted in the crush to get a glimpse of their majesties. The King and Queen also visited Limehouse Town Hall where they received a loyal address from the mayors of five East London municipalities. The shops between the New Globe pub (left) and the Guardian Angels church (1896) were colourfully decorated.

Jubilee decorations, Appian Road, Old Ford, 1935. At times of national rejoicing friends and neighbours will combine their talents to ensure that 'our street' has the best displays.

Coronation decorations in Rippoth Road, Old Ford, 1937. Following the death of King George V and the abdication of Edward VIII, it was once more time to acclaim a new sovereign, George VI who, with Queen Elizabeth (the late Queen Mother), was crowned in Westminster Abbey. Once more the neighbourhoods worked tirelessly to produce some astonishing displays whose magnificence can only be hinted at in these monochrome photographs.

Above and left: Coronation displays in Old Ford, 1937. Two houses in Parnell Road (above) and one in Lefevre Road (left) celebrate in style. In these grey streets, the colours appeared especially vivid.

Opposite above: Coronation decorations in Ruston Street, Old Ford, 1937. The houses have all but disappeared behind an extravaganza of red, white and blue.

Opposite below: HMS *Coronation*, a remarkable individual effort in Armagh Road, Old Ford. Post-war rebuilding has left few reminders of the neighbourhoods pictured in this sequence of views.

Catholic procession, Grundy Street by Prospect Place, Poplar, *c.* 1913. Religious processions on saint's days were a highlight of life in the streets of the East End when devout householders would set up shrines and altars which would be blessed by the priest as the parade passed by. Children from local Catholic schools enjoyed dressing up for the processions, and at dusk the candle-lit shrines made a pretty sight in the sometimes lavishly decorated streets. The parade here is passing a long-lost stretch of residential and commercial property at the western end of Grundy Street, where the shop window of baker Jack Brown has been adorned with religious pictures. Next door, Mrs Magdelia Bloom's dairy remained shuttered as was Solomon Cohen's fried-fish shop. Further along, wooden hoardings marked the demise of Thomas Skudder's beer shop.

An event of a different kind took place here in 1951 when a war-damaged area between Burdett Road and Chrisp Street was utilised for the Festival of Britain's Exhibition of Architecture which showcased post-war town planning and building design. There was a Festival Enclosure off Upper North Street while Grundy Street traversed a wider area of the exhibition with its new housing, schools and a re-sited Chrisp Street Market and shopping centre. The festival's legacy of bright new neighbourhoods was part of a larger area of regeneration called Lansbury, the building of which continued throughout the festival and afterwards.

East India Dock Road near Augusta Street, Poplar, *c.* 1913. Traffic on this busy highway had been displaced to make room for the Catholic procession, and Eliza Jane Pearce's Fancy Repository (left) had closed for the day.

Peace party, Spey Street, Poplar, 1919. Britain celebrated the peace which finally ended the horror years of the First World War, and as ever the East End rejoiced with traditional street parties like this one in Spey Street, a turning off St Leonard's Road.

Peace party, Kerbey Street neighbourhood, Poplar, 1919. The East End responded to the national euphoria in traditional style with colourful street events like this. This picture was part of a series produced by part-time photographer Thomas Mace who sold them at his sweetshop at No. 77 Kerbey Street.

A children's tea party, peace celebrations, 1919. In an unidentified street somewhere in the East End, the younger children enjoy their tea in the sun-lit street as mums and elder siblings look on.

Charabanc outing from the Ship public house, Poplar High Street, *c.* 1925. A century ago pubs of all types and styles were everywhere in the streets of the East End, each of them providing its own brand of good cheer and a focus of social life in the neighbourhood. Pubs often provided a starting point for outings, with attractions like Epping Forest and Southend-on-Sea proving popular in the East End. It was more likely that a group like the one pictured here was off to spend a day at the races, probably the Derby; on Derby Day horse-brakes and charabancs would descend on Epsom Downs from all over London. This crowd of day trippers have gathered outside George Anderson's Ship pub in Poplar High Street near Preston's Road, for one of the regular outings enjoyed by employees of the firm Vokins & Co. – general lightermen and lighterage contractors based at Poplar Docks and Pepper Warehouses, East India Dock Road. Next to the pub was Ernest Woodward's fried-fish shop which on this day may have picked up some late business from those wanting a fish supper when the party returned home.

The Railway Tavern (Charlie Brown's), West India Dock Road by Garford Street, *c.* 1905. Rare indeed is the pub whose proper name is all but forgotten in favour of that of its landlord, but a notable example once thrived in Limehouse. Charles Brown took over the running of the unremarkable Railway Tavern in 1893, and by sheer strength of personality turned it into a renowned establishment, famed far beyond the East End. Part of its success was due to a remarkable collection of curiosities and antiquities from all over the world which Charlie gradually accumulated, turning the tavern into an early example of a theme pub. Charlie was also an enormously popular character, a true East Ender who worked tirelessly fundraising for his favourite charities with contributions from those who came from afar to view his treasures. The photograph shows Charlie (front, in a straw boater) typically in party mood with a bus full of regulars setting off on a jolly outing, with a crowd of locals to see them on their way. The brightly painted bus would have attracted much attention, for these were the earliest days of motorised bus travel in London and for some of these people, this may have been their first trip in such a vehicle. It had been hired for the day from the London Motor Omnibus Co. whose fleet name 'Vanguard' would soon become familiar in London.

The Railway Tavern was rebuilt in 1919 by which time Charlie's son, Charlie Jnr, had taken over as landlord. When Charlie Brown died in 1932, he was given the sort of send-off the East End reserves for its greatest heroes, with the streets jammed with crowds anxious for a glimpse of Charlie's flower-decked funeral procession as it passed by.

Children's outing, Barking Road by Rathbone Market, Canning Town, *c.* 1906. A children's outing was a highlight in the lives of young East Enders and an escape from the sometimes wearisome streets of their neighbourhoods. Here, a huge gathering of excited youngsters clad in their Sunday best have piled aboard a fleet of horse-brakes in readiness for their trip to some salubrious spot for fun and games in the fresh air. The lower photograph shows the trippers passing St Margaret and All Saints Catholic church and schools, and the Women Workers' Settlement.

A trio of refreshment houses at the Norton Folgate end of Shoreditch High Street, *c.* 1906. The Crown & Shuttle pub was flanked by Uncle Tom's Cabin, a working man's cocoa, coffee and dining room of some fifty years' standing, while to the right Thomas Frank's Dining Rooms provided a good meal of sausage, mash and chips for 2½d.

Above: A typical East End pub: The Alexandra, Upper North Street by Pekin Street, Poplar, *c*. 1940. The modest scale of this cosy little 'local' matched that of the surrounding shops and houses – the public bar, on the left, had been created out of one of the houses. To the right, Harold Gander, who traded as an 'English hairdresser' ran The Olde Barber's Shoppe.

Right: The Cherry Tree, Brunswick Road by St Leonard's Road, Poplar, *c*. 1940. This solidly Victorian main-road pub sported a modernised ground floor, but the landlord's living space upstairs remained true to the original design.

Above: An East End beerhouse, Old Bethnal Green Road by Teesdale Street, *c.* 1905. George Robinson's premises have attracted a large assembly of local worthies who one hopes were still around when the premises were rebuilt in 1908 – in later years this became the Flower Pot pub. The photograph was by Arthur Griffiths (later Griffiths & Son), a company whose studios in Armagh Road, Old Ford, would be graced by generations of East Enders until their closure in the mid-1970s.

Left: The Cobden's Head, St Leonard's Road by Cobden Street, Poplar, *c.* 1912. Esther Chamberlin's modest premises featured a public bar and an area to which clients brought their own jugs to be filled with local brewer Mann, Crossman & Paulin's eternally popular refreshment.

Above left: Harry Hyam's Old Duke of Cambridge, Devons Road, Bromley-by-Bow, *c.* 1909.

Above right: The White Bear, St George Street by Breezer's Hill, Stepney, *c.* 1906.

Right: Henry Levy Steingold's Old George, Whitechapel Road, *c.* 1910.
(All courtesy of Maurice Friedman)

The Edinburgh Castle, Rhodeswell Road, Limehouse, c. 1906. With architectural features which reflected its name, this once rip-roaring gin palace acquired respectability and a new owner in 1873 when Thomas (Doctor) Barnardo reinvented it as a temperence working man's club and people's mission church.

Prince's Theatre (Poplar Hippodrome), East India Dock Road, c. 1906. Cinema-going was a popular leisure-time activity in the East End and as long ago as 1907 the showing of 'animated pictures' during live shows at the Poplar Hippodrome introduced East End audiences to the evolving entertainment medium. The theatre opened on Boxing Day, 1905, and is seen here soon afterwards – it became the Poplar Hippodrome in 1907 and a full-time cinema by the mid-1920s. The elegant residential terrace seen beyond the theatre included the Neptune Hotel which doubtless provided 'digs' for the theatre's visiting performers.

five

Aspects of East London

Rectory Square and East London synagogue, *c.* 1917. For centuries the East End has thrived as a cultural melting pot, its native cockneys joined by immigrants and settlers from many lands who all brought their lifestyles and traditions to the capital city. Protestant Huguenots from France came late in the seventeenth century, followed by Scandinavian, Oriental and Irish incomers, but it was the huge influx of Jewish people who joined a small existing Jewish population in the nineteenth century which gave the East End some of its most distinctive neighbourhoods. The Jews brought their religion and traditions and established a network of synagogues which ranged from modest house conversions to the Byzantine splendours of the East London synagogue which opened in Rectory Square in 1876. It was the first major synagogue in the East End and became notable for the memorials to the 700 Jewish soldiers who fought and died for Britain in the First World War. As the twentieth century progressed, the Jewish population in the East End declined and in 1987 the East London synagogue was sold and later reborn as Temple Court, a residential conversion. The picture shows neighbourhood children cultivating Rectory Square's garden – it is likely that vegetables were being grown during a period of wartime food shortage. The traditional terraced houses which once lined this oddly shaped 'square' have been rebuilt.

Opposite: Old Castle Street synagogue, Whitechapel, *c.* 1915. Far removed from the grandeur of the East London synagogue were the tiny neighbourhood places of worship which were to be found everywhere in the old Jewish ghettoes of the East End. Old Castle Street had a typical example, its entrance (seen to the right of the distant wagon) being a feature of an otherwise residential and commercial terrace. Neighbouring china and glass dealer Joseph Palkowski had a warehouse to the right and a corner shop by Wentworth Street in the far distance. (Courtesy of LMA)

Whitechapel library, *c.* 1904. Opened in 1901, the library was located in the culturally deprived neighbourhoods of Jewish Whitechapel. The new facility was welcomed with enthusiasm by youthful Jewry with a thirst for knowledge, and for some the library was styled 'the University of the Ghetto'. A blue wall plaque honours artist and poet Isaac Rosenberg, an East Ender who studied in the library. The adjacent Whitechapel Art Gallery (left) was built between 1897 and 1899.

Whitechapel Road and the Pavilion Theatre, *c.* 1902. With its Yiddish plays and cantorial concerts, the Pavilion was another centre of Jewish life in the East End and was also used as a synagogue on High Holy days. The theatre's life began in 1828, and following a series of rebuildings, finally closed in 1962.

Congregational chapel, Harley Street (Grove), Mile End, *c.* 1910. Worshippers from three faiths have gathered at this elegant building since its opening in 1830. The first change came in 1927 when the building emerged from alterations as the Mile End and Bow United synagogue, a role it fulfilled until 1977. A decline in Jewish and an increase in Asian populations led to the building's rebirth as a Sikh temple.

Christ Church, Spitalfields, *c.* 1905. Nicholas Hawksmoor's awesome Christ Church (1729) proclaimed the prosperity of Huguenot Spitalfields with a bold innovative design which towered high above the elegant neighbourhoods of weaver's and merchant's townhouses. (Courtesy of Maurice Friedman)

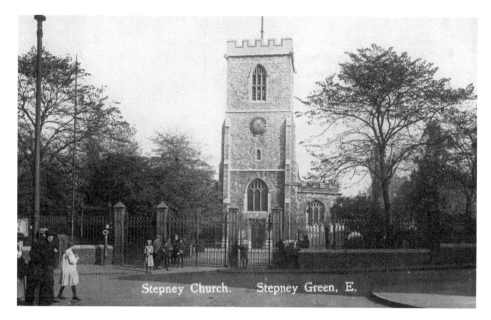

St Dunstan's, Stepney, *c.* 1914. When the Normans built the Tower of London in the eleventh century, the great fortress looked eastward over a green landscape containing a scattering of isolated settlements including *Stibenhede*, the future Stepney. Its Anglo-Saxon church has been rebuilt many times to meet the needs of the increasingly urbanised village as London expanded. War damage removed many surrounding streets but there has been a return to the greenery of old with the creation of the Stepping Stones urban farm.

St Mary, Stratford-le-Bow, *c.* 1875. Of medieval origin, the mostly seventeenth-century church was originally a chapel-of-ease to St Dunstan's, Stepney – it became a parish church in 1719. The westward-looking view catches an elegant neighbourhood of Georgian houses while tracks in the road were for the latest transport innovation – horse trams.

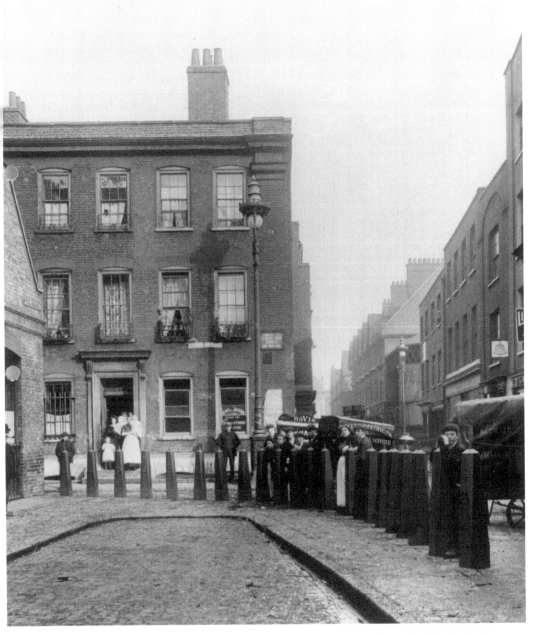

Spital Square by Church Passage, Spitalfields, *c.* 1909. Church Passage led to St Mary's church whose site was about to be claimed for extensions to the fruit market. The once grand mansion facing the camera was the last of three built in 1733 for wealthy merchants and having served time as a police station in the 1800s, it is seen here in multiple occupation before being lost to road widening in the 1920s. The view looks beyond a formidable battery of cast-iron bollards to the gabled buildings which came in 1893 with the reconstruction of Spitalfields, London's wholesale fruit and vegetable market. (Courtesy of LMA)

Left: St John's Charity School, Scandrett Street, Wapping, *c.* 1920. The school was founded in 1695 along a narrow lane which connected Wapping's riverside with a semi-rural hinterland of market gardens and pasture. Rebuilding in 1760 gave the children a fine new school which still stands alongside the old tower of St John's church, which itself replaced an earlier church in 1756. Both church and school buildings live on as residential conversions.

Below: St Stephen's Church of England Schools, Quaker Street, by Wheler Street, Spitalfields, *c.* 1908. The school opened in 1872, but problems caused by heavy road traffic and the proximity to Bishopsgate railway goods yard brought about a premature closure in 1909. The building proved more durable and still stands following its sale in 1929.

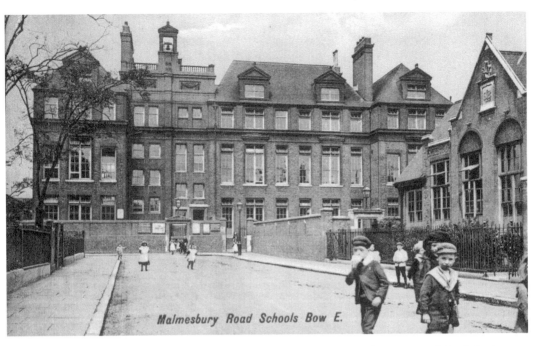

Malmesbury Road schools, Bow, *c.* 1906. The Junior School was built in 1884 and the Infant's School in 1899, both provided by the School Board for London in a style familiar throughout London – the Board was abolished in 1904. The writer of this postcard comments on the school's 'wretched red brick' and notes that half the school's pupils were Jewish in 1906.

Empire Day celebrations (later to become Commonwealth Day) at Malmesbury Road School, *c.* 1908. The flag added patriotic colour to the piano which accompanied the children's singing.

Whitechapel Primitive Methodist Mission, *c.* 1905 Sandwiched between Whitechapel Road Underground station (left) and the Rodney's Head pub, this fine building was home to an organisation set up in 1896 by the Revd Thomas Jackson to work for disadvantaged East End youth. Young offenders were given homes, training and a chance to emigrate to Canada and Australia – there were musical concerts held here on Saturday evenings to raise funds for the charitable work.

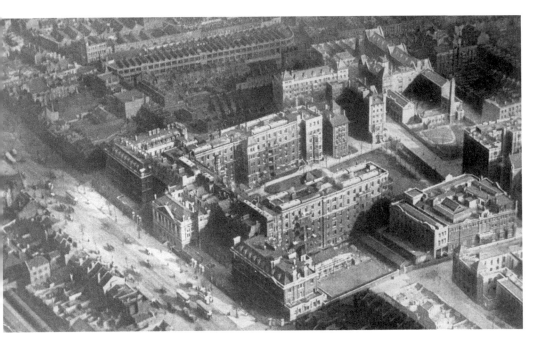

The London Hospital (The Royal London Hospital), Whitechapel Road, *c.* 1925. There has been a lifetime of healthcare here for generations of East Enders since the hospital's move to its present site in 1753. By 1876 the hospital had become the largest in the country and by the early 1900s had been likened to a small town with 'neighbourhoods' of its own.

The London Hospital training home for pupil probationers, Tredegar House, Bow Road, Mile End, *c.* 1912. This establishment fed a constant stream of trained nurses into the hospital, but here was a lighter moment with a genteel game of croquet for the trainees.

George Wallis, builder's supply merchant, Burdett Road, Mile End, c. 1928. Many East End homes benefited from the products made by this company during a lengthy trading period in Burdett Road from the 1890s to around 1970. The firm, which also supplied sanitary ware and ironmongery, expanded from its original base at No. 140 to other addresses in Burdett Road and Eric Street – Wallis's also had board mills alongside the local stretch of Regent's Canal. Here, an impressive fleet of delivery and other vehicles line up in Burdett Road, devoid of its usual dockland generated traffic, suggesting that this was a Sunday. Also revealed are the neighbouring premises of Barnet Rottenberg, ladies' tailor; Mrs Elizabeth Schultz, newsagent and a branch of the once prolific Stepney Laundry. All these buildings fronted once populous neighbourhoods which ran back to the Regent's Canal, an area since transformed by the creation of Mile End Park and the famous Green Bridge (1999) over Mile End Road.

Opposite above: George Wiseman, carman and haulage contractor, Poplar, c. 1888. The East End was an industrious quarter of the capital with many manufacturing plants and factories which gave employment to the considerable population. Small-scale businesses and service industries abounded, and in horse-drawn London, carmen provided essential delivery services. George Wiseman's cartage business operated from stables in an otherwise residential Langton Street, part of a neighbourhood later claimed for the post-war Bartlett Park.

Opposite below: Florida Street, Bethnal Green, c. 1896. In the East End's old silk-weaving neighbourhoods, houses like these were the live/work units of their day. The looms were placed upstairs to catch as much daylight as possible, while the family resided downstairs.

Bryant & May's match factory, Fairfield Works, Fairfield Road, Bow, *c.* 1920. There was a high concentration of matchmaking works in the East End, but the one founded by William Bryant and Francis May in 1861 to make the newly invented safety match was the largest. The works, seen here, was built in 1911 and dominated the neighbourhood, and although matchmaking ceased in 1971, the building lives on as residential Bow Quarter.

The Carmen's Caterer, No. 102 Whitechapel Road, *c.* 1906. Carmen were the delivery drivers and carriers of Victorian and Edwardian London, their horse-drawn vans and wagons a familiar sight everywhere, especially in commercially orientated areas like the East End. The work was arduous and generated hearty appetites so when it was time for a break, establishments like William (Bill) Rogers Dining Rooms were on hand with a substantial menu which was a cut above that provided by the basic 'pie and mash' emporia. Bill Rogers' family and staff have lined up here, while to the right, an Underground poster reveals the presence of what would become one of London's 'lost' Underground stations, St Mary's (Whitechapel). This Metropolitan & District Railway station, which was located on the line between Aldgate East and Whitechapel stations, served the community from 1884 to its closure in 1938. Also here from 1921 was the vast and opulent Rivoli cinema which succumbed to the Blitz in 1941. Number 102, Whitechapel Road still exists in a rebuilt state, but all traces of the station and cinema have been cleared away, and there is now a car showroom and the East London mosque (1985) to mark their sites.

Opposite below: Eastern district post office, Whitechapel Road, *c.* 1905 It was a proud day at East London's main postal sorting office with the arrival of a pioneering motor van. From 1927 this office became the eastern terminus of the unique Post Office Railway, a subterranean line which sped the mail between the six sorting offices it served. The line closed in 2003.

Above: Steam wagon accident, 1906. While many firms retained their horse-drawn delivery vehicles well into the twentieth century, others were more adventurous and experimented with newly evolving mechanical traction. Among them were brewers Harvey Greenfield & Co. (the Eagle Brewery) of Wellclose Square, but a spectacular mishap left their steam wagon poised terrifyingly above the Regent's Canal with only the barrel-laden trailer preventing it from plunging into the water below.

Left: Arcade Works, Back Church Lane, Whitechapel, *c.* 1918. The works occupied part of the former Peoples Arcade, a 'peoples retail market' built in 1906. Also known as Back Church Lane market, the complex had around 130 units from which mostly Jewish retailers catered to the domestic trade – fishmongers and poulterers predominated. Business, however, was poor and as customers dwindled away so did the tradesmen, and by 1910 only twenty-two remained. Inevitable closure followed with a long industrial afterlife for the building, which was still standing in the 1980s.

Pritchard's Road by Regent's Canal, Bethnal Green, *c.* 1903. Canals came about through a need to transport materials more efficiently in the pre-railway era when roads were poor. In East London the Limehouse Cut (1770) and Regent's Canal (1820) led the way, the latter going on to link the Thames with the national network of inland waterways. The canals attracted new industry and there were mixed commercial and residential neighbourhoods where a workforce was readily available. The picture shows a typical canal side neighbourhood with its small-scale industry – including Francis Church's scrap-iron yard at London Wharf, and William Porch's timber yard on the far bank of the Regent's Canal by Andrew's Road. Pritchard's Road itself ran on past George Rowe's fried-fish shop to Cat & Mutton Bridge where it entered The Broadway, now the trendy Broadway Market, London Fields. Although it is now overlooked by tower blocks, there is still a very real sense of the old East End here, with preserved terraces, shops and a vibrant local community. The Sir Walter Scott pub (left) is seen before its 1909 rebuilding – it is now a restaurant. By the late twentieth century, canal-side locations like this had become desirable places to live, and today a smart new complex of apartments, also called London Wharf, has replaced the scrap-metal yards of a century ago. (Courtesy of LMA)

Coke Loading

Retort House

The Commercial Gas Co. works, Harford Street, Stepney, *c.* 1920. The early nineteenth century saw the introduction of a revolutionary source of light and heat – gas. The first gas works in the East End began production (1814) in Wellclose Square with the much larger plant in Harford Street operational from 1838. The extensive site was bounded by the Regent's Canal where the Commercial Gas Co. had a wharf which allowed coal to be brought direct to the works by water. The coal had been shipped to Regent's Canal Dock from the Tyne by the company's own colliers and brought up to the works by barge. Movement of coal and coke within the works was undertaken by tiny Sharp Stewart locomotives (upper picture) – these could haul twenty-ton loads. One of the locomotives, which dated from 1895, was eventually sold for use in a pleasure ground, but it never actually entered service.

Opposite: The Commercial Gas Co. works, *c.* 1920. Further scenes at the works, including the company's wharf (top) with a sailing barge which had brought coal from the colliers in Regent's Canal Dock, Limehouse.

Unloading Craft

Trade Coke Loaders

Screen

Commercial Street, Spitalfields, 1907. The construction of Commercial Street in the 1840s and
'50s cut a swathe through the historic neighbourhoods between Norton Folgate, Bishopsgate
and Brick Lane, but usefully linked Shoreditch with the great east/west highways at Aldgate and
Whitechapel. In the early 1870s, horse-drawn tram cars were beginning to serve some of London's
main roads, but Commercial Street had to wait until 1888 for its tracks to be laid. The dawn of the
Edwardian age saw London's first electric trams, and in 1907 a photographer was on hand to record
the arrival of the first ones to serve Commercial Street where there was a healthy display of local
interest. The trams were of a highly advanced design and featured the luxury of a covered top deck;
nevertheless, Edwardian posteriors still had to contend with seating made of unyielding wooden
slats. On the left are some of the Victorian shops built to line the new Commercial Street while
behind them was the old Huguenot silk-weaving district. To the right was Spitalfields, London's
fruit and vegetable market whose origins can be traced back to 1682 when its license was granted
by Charles II. Its late-Victorian buildings were the result of a reconstruction by Robert Homer,
a one-time market porter who prospered to such an extent he acquired the market in 1856. The
Corporation of London purchased the market in 1920 and in 1991 the facility moved away to
outer London. It has since been revitalised as a visitor attraction with craft and collector's markets,
ethnic food outlets and trendy shops. (Courtesy of LMA)

Gardiner's Corner, Whitechapel, *c.* 1928. Multiple tramlines and heavy commercial traffic had to negotiate this complex junction at which traffic lights had yet to arrive. A tram inspector was on hand to control the various routes at the busiest times.

A trolleybus in East Smithfield by Dock Street terminus, *c.* 1958. The year 1940 saw the last of the Aldgate trams by which time East Enders were enjoying the latest ultra-modern electric transport, trolleybuses. These glided noiselessly along and might have been perceived as the ideal transportation for busy city streets, but all of them had gone by 1962 having had a shorter lifespan than their ancestors, the horse trams.

Aldgate High Street from Minories, *c.* 1913. Many elements of London's transport met at this eastern gateway to the City of London and are featured in this photograph which was taken by a French visitor to London. The viewpoint is from the open-top deck of a motorbus, an unrivalled position from which to survey the passing scene. The bus on the right was similar to the one on which the photographer was riding – it was one of the famous 'B' types, London's first standardised motorbus which finally replaced the last of the old horse buses. Similarly, a line of motor cabs on their rank in the centre of the road had all but replaced the hansoms and four-wheelers of Edwardian London. A line of electric trams in the far distance is close to Stepney's boundary with the City, whose Corporation steadfastly refused to allow electric transportation onto its streets except in three small localities. To the left is Aldgate Underground station which opened in 1876 when it was the terminus of the Metropolitan Railway. Another Underground sign further along marks Aldgate East station which opened in 1884 on the District Railway's extension line to New Cross. Wall lettering (centre) points the way to Haydon Square, one of the railway freight depots which existed around the outskirts of the City of London. Upon closure in 1962, Haydon Square's business was transferred to Broad Street.

Opposite below: A B-type bus, *c.* 1920. Despite their antiquated appearance, these buses were the 'Routemasters' of their day with many thousands of them making up a standardised fleet for the first time. The 'B's first appeared in 1910 and continued running until 1926. This one was working route 23 which was then a lengthy haul from Wormwood Scrubs to Rippleside, via Aldgate and Commercial Road.

A 'General' motorbus, *c.* 1910. Although London's first omnibuses appeared in 1829, it would be several years into the twentieth century before motorised examples would begin a regular service. This one arrived in 1909 and worked route 15, which still links London's East and West Ends via the City. The vehicle was operated by the London General Omnibus Co., forerunners of London Transport.

An RT-type bus, Aldgate station, *c.* 1949. This was the pre-war version of a London bus type which endured for many decades, and thanks to preservation societies can sometimes be spotted today. Part of the old Three Nuns Hotel is in the background.

An East End fog, *c.* 1975. London once had a reputation as a foggy city, and at a time when countless domestic coal fires and a vast array of smoking industrial chimneys poured out clouds of noxious vapours, the city was often enveloped in thick yellow fog for days at a time. The Clean Air Act (1956) cleared the worst of the visible pollution, but the odd foggy day recalled the horrors of old, as seen here with a Limehouse-bound RT-type bus looming through the murk. (Courtesy of David Brewster)

Opposite above: An East End outing, *c.* 1925. It is the mid-1920s and although London's buses were becoming larger and more comfortable, they had yet to feature such luxuries as covered top decks and pneumatic tyres. Nevertheless, these East Enders on their jolly day out seemed pleased with their S-type bus, on hire for the day from the London General Omnibus Co. (Courtesy of David Brewster)

Opposite below: Aldgate High Street, *c.* 1952. Trolleybuses and other traffic compete for road space in what has for centuries been a highly congested thoroughfare. The photograph also reveals a post-war legacy of patched-up buildings, including the truncated spire of the church of St Mary Matfelon which was damaged by lightning and later in the Blitz. The clock tower of Gardiner's department store survived the war but not the fire which would destroy it in May 1972.

Shadwell and St Georges East station, *c.* 1949. One of the East End's first passenger railways, the London and Blackwall, opened in 1840 and ran on a lengthy viaduct above the streets of Shadwell and Limehouse, giving local people a new perspective on their neighbourhoods. Shadwell's station opened in 1840 and closed in 1941 – it presented a dismal sight during its period of closure before the innovative Docklands Light Railway revived its fortunes in 1987.

Shoreditch station, 1955. London's Underground is the oldest subterranean passenger railway in the world, its original line from Paddington to Farringdon Street (1863) the tiny nucleus from which today's vast London-wide system grew. The East End was first served by the Underground in 1876 when the Metropolitan Railway was extended from Liverpool Street to Aldgate where it terminated, and although Shoreditch station also opened in 1876, it was not used by Metropolitan trains on the East London Line until 1913. From Shoreditch, the railway runs southwards connecting the densely populated neighbourhoods off Brick Lane with the riverside communities at Wapping, from where the line descends into the Thames Tunnel before emerging at Rotherhithe. Brunel's pioneering Thames Tunnel, which opened to pedestrians in 1843, was adapted for railway use in 1869. Shoreditch station (which is actually in Bethnal Green) is pictured here on an icy day with one of the Metropolitan's distinctive F-class trains, a reminder of the days when all Underground trains bore the all-red London Transport livery. To the left is the derelict southbound platform which fell out of use in 1941 in favour of a single platform arrangement. At the time of writing, Shoreditch station is a remarkable backwater on the Underground system, its cottage-like building still sporting a wooden floor. It only opens during weekday rush hours, but ambitious plans to upgrade and extend the East London Line are set to transform this Victorian transport relic. (Courtesy of Alan A. Jackson)

Opposite below: Bishopsgate goods station, Shoreditch, *c.* 1890. Built from 1877-82 on the historic site of the Eastern Counties Railway's 'London' station (1840), the Great Eastern Railway's freight terminal was one of the great railway landmarks of the East End until fire destroyed it in 1964. The Victorian's generous provision of street toilets (foreground) contrasts with their paucity today.

Coborn Road station, Bow, *c.* 1905. Opened in 1883 to replace an earlier station (1863), the Great Eastern Railway's Coborn Road station offered a quick journey into Liverpool Street, its pair of widely separated entrances in Grove Road and Coborn Road enabling the station to serve a good spread of neighbourhoods. The station closed in 1946.

Old Ford station, *c.* 1905. The North London Railway's services usefully linked Hackney, Bow and Poplar from a station in Old Ford Road which was in use from 1867 to 1944. The station buildings were removed in the 1960s, and the landscape hereabouts has been much altered by major road building.

Above and below: First World War air-raid damage, 1916. In a country which had grown unused to fighting its wars on home soil, the First World War brought an unfamiliar terror to all Londoners as advancing technology reached the point where the death and destruction of the battlefield could be delivered into anyone's local neighbourhood. The first raids on London came in 1916 from Zeppelin airships – these were joined in 1917 by Gotha bombers which brought daylight raids for the first time. These postcards by Poplar photographer William Whiffen attempt to convey the horror of it all in Botolph Road, Bow (above), and an un-named road in Old Ford (below).

Above and below. Communities in the East End, as elsewhere, celebrated a safe deliverance from the trauma of the First World War only for an appalling fate to befall them during the twentieth century's second great conflict. In the upper picture Canning Town's Ravenscroft Road is seen during Peace Day celebrations in 1919 but the lower photograph from the Second World War tells a different story.

The Nag's Head, Whitechapel Road, c. 1941. Life in the East End continued as best it could during the air raids of two world wars, and an indomitable cockney spirit meant it was usually 'business as usual' in the face of extreme adversity. Here, a typical East End pub lay devastated by the Blitz, but long-serving landlord Joseph Perkoff ensured his regulars did not go thirsty at what remained of his premises. The pub was rebuilt after the war.

Above and below: The Victory Parade, 1946. The 1940s was the grimmest decade in the East End with the constant threat of air raids eventually replaced by post-war austerity and rationing of household essentials. With the war finally at an end in 1945, peace brought a period of euphoria with street parties and an impressive Victory Parade. This took in the East End along a lengthy route from Regent's Park to The Mall where the King and Queen saluted the mechanised divisions of the armed services, and prominent war leaders as they passed by. The parade is seen passing the Museum cinema, Cambridge Heath Road, Bethnal Green (above) and a war-scarred Tower Hill (below).

The aftermath of war: Prefabs in Poplar, 1947. With its destruction of entire neighbourhoods by enemy action, the Second World War left a desperate housing shortage in its wake. The crisis led to the introduction of revolutionary prefabricated housing (prefabs) which could be erected quickly on cleared sites creating clean modern accommodation which was often an improvement on some of the old terraced houses it replaced. The prefabs were popular as East Enders turned them into warm comfortable homes, and although they were intended as a temporary measure, a few prefabs lingered on towards the end of the century. Corrugated iron Nissen huts were also pressed into service, but their tunnel-shaped space made them less appealing, as did their metal roofs which made them uncomfortably hot in summer. Both types of accommodation were represented on this estate of temporary housing, which arose on the sites of a dense grid of Victorian streets which included Latham Street, Lindfield Street, Cottall Street and Upper North Street. Stainsby Street is in the foreground and the heavy industry on the horizon was by the Limehouse Cut. These temporary neighbourhoods were soon cleared but in 1959 even more transitory ones took their place as a vast travellers' encampment appeared, but even in the midst of that chaotic jumble of caravans and scrap metal, the old street pattern survived. This was, however, the last of the old community and today a new green lung, Bartlett Park, covers the old sites together with a lone survivor, St Saviour's church, Northumbria Street, known today as the Celestial Church of Christ. (Courtesy of LMA)

Other local titles published by The History Press

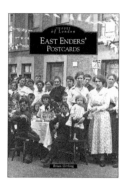

East Enders' Postcards
BRIAN GIRLING

This selection of old views from the capital city's East End combines popular sights with everyday scenes; from aerial views of Tower Bridge and London Docks to vistas of terraced houses, shops and businesses, as well as trams, streets and buildings which have long since disappeared. Images of King George V's Silver Jubilee celebrations in 1935, along with markets at Brick Lane, reflect the traditional community spirit for which this area of London is renowned.

0 7524 2494 7

Bethnal Green
GARY HAINES

This collection of over 200 old photographs takes a broad view of the history of Bethnal Green, presenting a reflective account of the area from the earliest references, through its notorious nineteenth-century period and over the subsequent regenerative changes to the present day. *Bethnal Green* provides a valuable account for the long-time resident, and further makes the history of the area and its people both accessible and alive for the interested newcomer today.

0 7524 2677 X

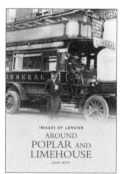

Around Poplar and Limehouse
GAVIN SMITH

This pictorial history traces some of the changes that have taken place in Poplar and Limehouse during the last century, and also looks at the histories of some of the surrounding communities, including Wapping, Millwall and Blackwall. With over 170 illustrations this collection highlights some of the important events that have occurred in this part of East London during this time, and captures the essence of the area's maritime heritage and its shipping industry.

0 7524 3222 2

London: Life in the Post-War Years
DOUGLAS WHITWORTH

These evocative images of London were taken in the years immediately following the Second World War and are the work of Douglas Whitworth who took many photographs of people, places and events in the capital during this period. The pictures capture the atmosphere of the time, and also feature a succession of nostalgic views around some of London's most famous streets and landmarks, including Petticoat Lane and Speaker's Corner.

0 7524 2816 0

If you are interested in purchasing other books published by The History Press, or in case you have difficulty finding any of our books in your local bookshop, you can also place orders directly through our website
www.thehistorypress.co.uk